This Jo

Published by

Real Joy Publications

Made in the USA
Monee, IL
16 March 2023

29995706R00066